BE

STRONG

IN THE

LORD

PRAYING FOR THE
ARMOR OF GOD
FOR YOUR CHILDREN

BE STRONG IN THE LORD

PRAYING FOR THE ARMOR OF GOD FOR YOUR CHILDREN

Betsy Duffey and Laurie Myers

Writing Sisters Press

Atlanta, Georgia

Cover by Berge Design

Writing Sisters Press, Atlanta, Georgia

ISBN-13: 978-1536841046
ISBN-10: 1536841048

SDG

The Armor of God

Finally, be strong in the Lord
and in the strength of his might.

Put on the whole armor of God, that you may be able to
stand against the schemes of the devil.

Stand therefore, having fastened on the belt of truth,
and having put on the breastplate of righteousness,
and, as shoes for your feet, having put on the readiness
given by the gospel of peace.

In all circumstances take up the shield of faith, with which
you can extinguish all the flaming darts of the evil one;

and take the helmet of salvation, and the sword of the
Spirit, which is the word of God,

praying at all times in the Spirit, with all prayer and
supplication. To that end keep alert with all perseverance,
making supplication for all the saints,

and also for me, that words may be given to me in
opening my mouth boldly to proclaim the mystery of the
gospel, for which I am an ambassador in chains,
that I may declare it boldly, as I ought to speak.

Ephesians 6:10-11, 14-20

CONTENTS

INTRODUCTION

We long for our children to be safe and secure in a dangerous world. We invest in security systems for our homes. We buckle our children into car seats. But are they safe? In a world that is unsafe, God provides protection by giving us his equipment for security: the armor of God.

The Apostle Paul describes the armor of God in the book of Ephesians. It's thought that he wrote the passage while under arrest in Rome, chained to a Roman soldier. He was very familiar with the Roman soldier's armor. As he looked at the physical armor that protected the soldiers, he described the spiritual armor that our children need.

The belt, breastplate, shoes, shield, helmet, and sword keep the soldier safe and make him an effective opponent in battle. Paul describes spiritual tools: truth, righteousness, faith, service, salvation, scripture, and prayer. God provides these for our children's safety and well-being. The armor makes all the difference.

Like the armor that protects a soldier, God's spiritual armor protects our children. He provides everything they need to live and thrive in a hostile world. You can pray for your children to have this protection.

1

GIVE THEM STRENGTH

Our children need God's strength.

Be strong in the Lord and in the strength of his might.

We want our children to be strong. We give them vitamins and nutritious food. We make sure they have medical checkups and regular dental exams. We pay a lot of attention to their physical bodies, but what about their hearts and souls? How can we strengthen them for life?

The Roman army was the strongest in the world. It was made up mainly of Roman citizens who volunteered for service. Behind each soldier was a structure of command that supported and directed him.

A legion of four thousand men was divided into cohorts, which were broken down into centuria, all made up of individual soldiers, totally committed to Rome. Each man on his own was weak and powerless compared to the strength he experienced when he was linked to his army and commander.

Roman soldiers came from all walks of life, but they had one thing in common: they were committed. They had aligned themselves with Rome and had allegiance to their country and to their commanding officer. Behind each soldier was a larger power.

Just as each soldier aligned himself to something bigger and more powerful, our children must look beyond their own strength and align themselves with the power and might of God. Our children are weak and vulnerable alone, but when they join the army of God they have power in his strength. When we join with God to support and grow our children, we tap into his power and strength on their behalf. We raise children who are strong in the Lord.

- Our children need God's strength to protect their hearts and souls.

- When our children align themselves with God, he provides the power that they need for their protection and wellbeing.

- As parents and caring adults in a child's life we can join with God to empower them to be strong in him.

May you be strengthened with all power, according to his glorious might, for all endurance and patience with joy.

COLOSSIANS 1:11

Mighty God,

You have promised us your strength, and that we can be strong in you. Through your love, you have provided a way for
_____ and _____ to live a good life, safe in your care, empowered to do your work.

Show me how I can join you in equipping _____
and _____ to be strong and to know you, their Commander.

Let me lead them into an understanding of your strength and ways in the world.

Grow my faith that I can be a mighty soldier in your ranks. Teach me about you so that I can teach _____ and
_____ .

Thank you for providing a way for us to follow you without fear, whatever we encounter in this world.

Help our children to be strong in your power.

Amen

❖

I can do all things through him who strengthens me.

PHILIPPIANS 4:13

2

EQUIP THEM

God equips our children to defend themselves.

Put on the whole armor of God

We would do anything to protect our children, but our efforts can only go so far. The troubles of this world will come: natural disaster, disease, war. Children are young, vulnerable, and defenseless to deal with these troubles ... unless they have the armor of God and learn to put it on.

When a Roman soldier prepared for battle, he started with his linen undergarment, then his wool tunic, cinched up with a short rope to make a skirt.

The heavy breastplate was lifted onto his shoulders, usually with help, and was tied into place. The belt was buckled around the waist, pulling in the woolen fabric of the tunic, the breastplate, and the buckler for the sword.

Then the soldier was ready to put on the helmet and take up his shield and sword.

The armor was provided by Rome, but each soldier had to take it up and put it on. Each piece was essential for his protection and success. He had to recognize the value and importance of each piece of armor, and choose to put it on each day.

Just like a soldier needs his protective armor, our children need protection. God has provided all the armor and weapons our children need: truth, righteousness, faith, service, salvation, scripture, and prayer. The systematic putting on of the armor every day gives a child protection from the obstacles that they will encounter. They must recognize the importance of each piece and choose to put it on.

- Without God's protection, our children are vulnerable against their enemies.

- God provides spiritual armor for our children: truth, righteousness, faith, service, salvation, scripture, and prayer.

- As parents and caring adults in a child's life we can teach them about the tools available to help them stand firm in a corrupt world.

fear not, for I am with you;
be not dismayed, for I am your God;
I will strengthen you, I will help you,
I will uphold you with my righteous right hand.

ISAIAH 41:10

Dear Lord,

I know that as much as I love my children I cannot protect them from the world. Give me peace as I surrender them to your care. Protect _____ and _____ in your strength. You alone can save and protect them.

Give _____ and _____ your armor, and give them the ability and courage to take it up and put it on every day. Show them your truth, righteousness, faith, service, salvation, scripture, and prayer.

Today, guide _____ and _____ in your ways. Teach them the tools that will give them safety and wellbeing.

Each day as they put on your armor, strengthen them and give them wisdom and knowledge.

Thank you, Lord, for loving us and protecting us by giving us your armor. Thank you that you empower us to live fully and courageously in this dangerous world.

Amen

❖

The night is far gone; the day is at hand.
So then let us cast off the works of darkness
and put on the armor of light.

ROMANS 13:12

3

SHOW THEM TRUTH

Our children need to know the truth.

Stand therefore, having fastened on the belt of truth

The first time we hear our child lie we are amazed. As we confess to other parents that our child lied, we learn that we are not alone! Lies make other sins possible. The first line of protection for our children is truth. They need to learn to put it on like a belt.

The soldier's belt was a strong leather strap, often reinforced with metal plates. It circled the waist, and held the rest of the armor together.

Without it the other pieces, including the breastplate, hung loose, unable to function. The belt strengthened and supported the soldier's body.

Before battle the soldier would pick up the hem of the tunic and tuck it up into his belt, giving him more mobility and freedom.

The belt also provided a place for the soldier to hang his weapons. It's no wonder that Paul listed the belt first, giving primary importance to truth.

Like a soldier needs a belt, our children need truth. God's truth strengthens and supports them, holding all aspects of their lives together. Without truth the rest of the armor is useless, and our children are defenseless against the lies and deceptions of the enemy. Lies, both big and small, destroy lives. A life bound together with truth has tremendous power to resist temptation.

- Our children need to build a foundation of truth, which enables them to use other weapons effectively.

- God provides the truth to our children, working in their hearts to make them love truth more than lies.

- As parents and caring adults in a child's life we can model an honest life for them, and teach them the importance of being truthful.

and you will know the truth,
and the truth will set you free.

JOHN 8:32

Dear God,

Buckle the belt of truth around _____ and
_____ each day, holding their world together.
Make them people of integrity, speaking the truth in all situations.

Remind _____ and _____ that
you love truth, and that they can be people who love truth and hate
lies.

Show them the truth about you. You are great and mighty, slow to
anger, loving.

Let _____and _____ know your
promises: that you love them with an everlasting love, that you made
them in your image, that they are precious in your sight.

Help our children to put on the belt of truth, that they may stand
secure in you. Teach me your truths, Lord, so that I can teach them
to my children.

Thank you for revealing to us what is true and exposing to us what is
false.

Amen

❖

Lead me in your truth and teach me,
for you are the God of my salvation;
for you I wait all the day long.

PSALM 25:5

4

BE THEIR RIGHTEOUSNESS

Our children need God's righteousness to restore them.

having put on the breastplate of righteousness

Our children have tender hearts. Often they want to do right, but find themselves doing the very thing they know is wrong. Righteousness is doing what is right in the eyes of God, and our children can not do that on their own. They need the righteousness of God to protect their hearts and souls from sin and sorrow.

The breastplate was an important part of a Roman soldier's armor, protecting vital organs, like the heart and lungs. It was made of iron or chain mail, which made it heavy and cumbersome.

The breastplate covered the soldier's upper body and back. The belt allowed the weight of the breastplate to rest on the soldier's hips. When it was in place the soldier was protected.

Enemy weapons that got through the other defenses were stopped by the breastplate. Without a breastplate a soldier's heart was vulnerable to harm.

Like the soldier's heart must be protected by the breastplate, our children's hearts must be protected by God's righteousness, and that is not possible under their own power. In fact, it is frightening to think about them fighting with their own righteousness. Isaiah tells us that our righteousness is like "filthy rags". That's not much protection.
How do our children get that righteousness? By becoming a child of God. By following his commands. By seeking his counsel. With God's righteousness our children have a strong protection from the sword thrusts of the enemy.

- Children need God's restoring power. They must put their faith in him and not in their own abilities.

- God alone is perfect and righteous. He gives that righteousness to us.

- As parents and caring adults in a child's life, we can give them hope that when they fall short they have the righteousness of the one who is perfect.

Create in me a clean heart, O God,
and renew a right spirit within me.

PSALM 51:10

Father God,

Put your breastplate of righteousness on _____
and _____ , protecting their hearts. You know
their faults and love them unconditionally.

Grow _____ and _____ in grace
and wisdom as they trust you, and look to you for their guidance.

You alone can heal the sorrows that they feel when they fall short of
the way that is right.

Protect them from a world that encourages them to strive under their
own power, meeting the goals that the world dictates.

Keep their hearts tender and protected as they grow.

Thank you for giving us your righteousness when we believe in you.
Help me to put on your breastplate to guard my own heart.

Accept this prayer for _____ and
_____ and for me.

Amen

❖

And the peace of God, which surpasses all understanding,
will guard your hearts and your minds in Christ Jesus.

PHILIPPIANS 4:7

5

HELP THEM STAND

Our children need God's help to stand firm.

that you may be able to stand.

We love to see our children be confident: open to share what they know, take correction with grace, and meet life with optimism. But sometimes they are knocked down by difficulties - a death or disappointment. They need a firm foundation to help them stand.

Paul tells us four times to stand firm, so this must be critical. For soldiers, athletes, and dancers the stance is everything. This posture of strength shows confidence, and keeps them from being knocked off balance.

The Roman soldier's sandals were studded through the soles with heavy nails. Many studs or hobnails were in each shoe. They acted like cleats, and gave the soldier traction, making him sure-footed and able to stand strong against blows in battle.

With his shoes planted firmly in the ground he was hard to knock down. As the army advanced and took territory, their shoes continued to dig in, holding ground.

The Roman armor was not designed for one thing ... retreat. The soldier was vulnerable if he turned his back on the enemy.

Our children face uncertainties in life. Circumstances can make them feel off balance and unstable. Like the soldier needs solid shoes, our children need a solid foundation so that they can stand firm. They need to understand the assurances they have in God for protection and victory.

- Our children need God to stand with confidence.

- God's armor - truth, righteousness, faith, service, salvation, scripture, and prayer - imparts to our children an unflappable confidence.

- As parents and caring adults in a child's life we should encourage our children's confidence in God and in his protection.

For freedom Christ has set us free;
stand firm therefore, and do not submit again
to a yoke of slavery.

GALATIANS 5:1

Dear Heavenly Father,

My children will face times in life when they want to retreat. Give
_____ and _____ the strength to
stand firm in the confidence that they are loved and protected by
you.

Like the Roman soldier, help _____ and
_____ to plant themselves in solid ground.

Give them a firm foundation of faith to sustain them.

Life is scary and I admit that sometimes I want to run. Give me your
strength to withstand the challenges of life, so that I can be a good
example to _____ and _____.

Give us confidence as we stand firm with you. Standing with you, we
do not need to be afraid. You are stronger than any enemy that we
might face.

Thank you for protecting us in this world.

Amen

❖

Be watchful, stand firm in the faith, act like men, be strong.

1 CORINTHIANS 16:13

6

MAKE THEM READY

Our children should be ready to serve and to share the gospel.

as shoes for your feet,
having put on the readiness given by the gospel of peace.

Our children have different shoes for different occasions: sandals, dress up, rain, ballet, hiking, football. The right shoes make them ready to participate, and give them support. Our children need to be ready to share the good news of God's love.

Footwear was essential for a Roman soldier. His shoes were leather, laced around the ankle and up the leg. The soles were spiked so they would not slip and slide, and thick to protect from sharp hazards planted in the road by the enemy. Shoes had to be long-lasting, strong, and able to stand up under rocky terrain.

Only 20% of the soldier's job was fighting, the other 80% was making roads, walls, and forts.

Roman soldiers built over 25,000 miles of roads.

Shoes were valuable, and made the soldier ready for any situation that he would encounter.

Paul tells us that the right footwear is the gospel of peace. Gospel means good news. Like the soldier's shoes, knowing the good news about Jesus strengthens our children with a secure footing. When they share their belief about the love of Jesus, they can see the power of God working in the life of another person and in themselves.

- When our children know what they believe and are sure in their faith, they are strong enough to serve others and share their faith.

- God loved us so much that he sent his son, Jesus, to die for us, and in that certainty our children are ready to serve.

- As parents and caring adults we can convey to our children the security that comes from the knowledge of God's love through Jesus.

How beautiful upon the mountains
are the feet of him who brings good news,
who publishes peace, who brings good news of happiness,
who publishes salvation, who says to Zion, "Your God reigns."

ISAIAH 52:7

Dear God,

Give your peace to _____ and _____
so that they can be ready to serve others and to share the message of
your love. As they generously build the faith of others, build their
faith too.

Let them become comfortable with their knowledge of you, like a
pair of well fitting shoes. As _____ and
_____ grow, let them always be ready to tell others
about their faith and confidence in you.

Show me your love today, and help me to understand the good news
of Jesus in deep and fresh ways.

 Help me to be ready to serve you and to tell others the good news.

Thank you for this time to pray for _____
and_____ .

I know how much you love them.

Amen

❖

Peace I leave with you; my peace I give to you.
Not as the world gives do I give to you.
Let not your hearts be troubled,
neither let them be afraid.

JOHN 14:27

7

BUILD THEIR COMMUNITY

Our children need Christian friends and mentors.

In all circumstances take up the shield of faith

Our children need friends and mentors with whom they can link shields for protection. The world is a hostile place, and friends can help our children stay safe.

There were two kinds of shields that the Roman soldier used: a small round shield that he used in hand to hand combat, and a larger shield used for protection. Paul refers to the soldier's large shield when he describes the armor.

This shield completely covered the soldier. It was referred to as a door. It was the shape of a door, and to get to the soldier you had to go through it. This was the soldier's first line of defense. Soldiers would link their shields together to form a unified front as they faced the enemy. Sometimes they would link the shields over their heads to form a roof of protection. This formation was described as a turtle.

The soldier's shield was strong on its own, but when linked together with other shields it formed a stronger wall of protection, allowing the soldiers to be safe and to advance.

Our children need to know other people who are strong in faith so that they can link shields with them. With God surrounding our children, and good friends and family helping to shield them, we can rest in the knowledge that they are well protected.

- Our children need God's protection like a shield around them.

- Surrounding our children with others who are also raising their shields of faith can give added protection.

- As loving parents and caring adults in a child's life, we should help them build healthy relationships with mentors and faithful friends.

But you, O Lord, are a shield about me,
my glory, and the lifter of my head.

PSALM 3:3

Dear Lord,

You have told us that you are our shield. You surround us and keep us safe from our enemies. Be a shield for _____ and _____. Protect them against the dangers of life.

Give them good friends who share their faith and will help to protect them. Show _____ and_____ how to use their faith to make them strong and secure.

As they move through life continue to surround them with faithful mentors and friends.

Thank you for your promises of protection. Help me to build my own faith so that I can link shields with _____ and_____ to make a strong front against all enemies.

Like a shield keeping harm out, protect us. Thank you for your protection, and for giving us other people in our lives to join with us in faith.

Amen

❖

"Fear not, Abram, I am your shield;
your reward shall be very great."

GENESIS 15:1

8

GROW THEIR FAITH

Our children need faith to combat discouragement.

*take up the shield of faith, with which you can extinguish
all the flaming darts of the evil one.*

Children don't need to be taught that they have enemies, they sense it from a young age. There is the monster in the closet, something scary under the bed, a thing in the dark. Not everyone has the child's best interest in mind. Children can be excluded by peers or mocked and teased.

Roman soldiers needed protection against flaming darts. These were arrows that had been dipped in pitch and set on fire. The enemy would shoot the arrows into the air, raining them down on the soldiers.

The Romans were the first to learn to make a curved shield. The shield wrapped around the soldier, protecting him from many angles. But what about the flames?

The shield was covered in layers of leather. Before a soldier went into battle he soaked his shield in water. The fiery arrows would hit the shield and be put out. As long as the shield was wet, the arrows could not hurt.

God promises in scripture that he is our shield. Unfair criticism and discouraging comments wound our children, like flaming arrows. Faith protects them by constantly reminding them of who they are and who God is. God's love is like the water that wets the shield, extinguishing the pain of the comments before they can do damage.

- Our children will experience hurtful words in their lives.

- When unfair comments come, faith protects children, making them strong in the knowledge of who they are in the eyes of God.

- We can help our children withstand flaming arrows by reminding them of their faith, and encouraging opportunities to build faith.

You are my hiding place and my shield;
I have put my hope in your word.

PSALM 119:114

Lord,

Give your shield of faith to _____ and
_____, making them strong enough to withstand
lies that come to hurt them. Critical comments and taunts can be
painful. Shield our children from the flaming arrows that may come
their way.

When critical comments come to_____ and
_____ , give them discernment to know when to
accept the remarks and change.

When the flaming arrows that they encounter are lies, make them
strong in their faith and give them wisdom.

Help me to build their faith so that _____ and
_____ can stand firm. Give me the shield too, so
that I will not be thrown off by the lies of others.

Thank you for loving us and offering us this protection.

Amen

❖

The Lord is my rock and my fortress and my deliverer,
my God, my rock, in whom I take refuge,
my shield, and the horn of my salvation, my stronghold.

PSALM 18:2

9

PROTECT THEIR MINDS

Our children's minds need protection.

take the helmet of salvation

We all know the importance of a helmet. As our children go out to ride bikes or skateboard, we want that protection for their heads. But what about spiritual protection for their thoughts?

The Roman helmet protected the soldier's head. It was made with thick leather covered with metal plates, or made from bronze that had been molded or beaten into shape.

Metal helmets were lined with felt or sponge. It had cheek plates hanging down to protect the soldier's face, and came down in back to protect the neck. A soldier would never enter battle without the protection of his helmet.

Unlike some of the other pieces of armor, the helmet was only worn during a battle. Protecting the soldier's ability to reason and think was crucial, making the helmet a vital piece of armor.

In the same way that a soldier needs his head protected from injury, our children need their minds protected from damaging images and negative thoughts. Many battles against temptation are fought in our children's minds. God promises protection when they know him and follow his ways.

- Our children need right thinking to live and thrive in a corrupt world.

- God cares about our children's thoughts, and will protect them.

- As parents and caring adults in our children's lives, we can help them focus on good and worthy thoughts and banish negative thoughts.

Do not be conformed to this world,
but be transformed by the renewal of your mind,
that by testing you may discern what is the will of God,
what is good and acceptable and perfect.

ROMANS 12:2

Dear Lord,

Put the helmet of salvation on_____ and
_____ , to protect their thoughts and emotions.
Keep their minds focused on positive thoughts leading to positive
actions.

May _____ and _____ think
your thoughts and live good lives in confidence and faith.

Each day let them meditate on things that are true, right, noble,
excellent, and praiseworthy. May _____ and
_____ be protected from negative thoughts that
lead them to doubt you or their identity as your child.

Guard them against temptation that begins as an idea and grows into
negative actions.

Thank you for the safety that you give to our children.

Amen.

❖

*We destroy arguments and every lofty opinion
raised against the knowledge of God,
and take every thought captive to obey Christ*

2 CORINTHIANS 10:5

10

LET THEM KNOW YOU

Our children need to know and experience God.

take the helmet of salvation

The senses connect our children to the world. Their eyes take pictures - images that are both good and bad. A scented candle can make their homes warm and inviting. Opening a refrigerator to the smell of something spoiled can alert them to danger. Hearing and speech enable them to socialize and communicate. The senses are essentials for children to live a full and safe life.

The Roman soldier's helmet had a brow ridge to protect the eyes, and cheek plates to protect the ears and sides of the face.

A soldier used all his senses in battle. His vision was important to locate the enemy and keep sight of his commander. His ears heard the trumpets and commands that directed him in battle. His hand gripped the sword and felt its strength.

In the victory parade after a successful battle, incense was burned, giving a sweet smell as the soldiers marched into Rome. The soldiers feasted on good food and drink after their victory.

The sights and sound of battle, the feel of the strong armor, the smells and tastes of victory - all were important to the life of the soldier.

It is important that our children use their senses to experience God and to interact with the world around them.

- Children need quiet places, away from the noisy world, to hear God.
- Children need to see God's presence in the world through his creation and presence in others.
- Children need to be a fragrant aroma to God, experiencing him through serving.

He who has ears to hear, let him hear.

MATTHEW 11:15

. . . through us spreads the fragrance
of the knowledge of him everywhere.

2 CORINTHIANS 2:14

Oh, taste and see that the Lord is good!
Blessed is the man who takes refuge in him!

PSALM 34:8

Lord,

We long to know you and to experience your love. Allow
_____ and _____ to experience you
and your world through all of their senses.

Let our children hear you. Put the helmet over their ears so that they
may hear and obey the voice of the Lord.

Make they be able to experience the fragrance of the Lord that they
may be pleasing to him.

Pull the helmet down to protect our children's eyes so that they can
see through the eyes of Jesus. Help _____ and
_____ to keep their eyes on you.

Let them taste your Word and see that it is good.

May the words of our children's mouths and the meditations of their
hearts may be acceptable in your sight, O Lord, our Strength and our
Redeemer.

Amen

❖

And walk in love, as Christ loved us

and gave himself up for us,

a fragrant offering and sacrifice to God.

EPHESIANS 5:2

11

TEACH THEM YOUR WORD

Our children need the Word of God.

and the sword of the Spirit, which is the word of God.

The world bombards our children with disturbing images and ideas. It can be frightening without the assurance that someone bigger and more powerful is in control. Our children can combat those fears with the truth in scripture.

The sword is different from the other pieces of armor listed in these passages. It is the only offensive weapon. The soldier wore the sword in a scabbard attached to his belt. It was short, double sided, and had a handle that fit securely in the soldier's hand.

The Roman sword, called the gladius, was a close range weapon that was drawn during close combat. Its sharp double edges allowed the soldier twice the power, and its sharp point could pierce the enemy's heavy armor. Its light weight made it easy to handle. Without the sword the soldier was protected, but could not advance. No victories were possible without the sword.

The Bible may be the single most important weapon that a child has to live a life of resilience and strength. With the Word the child has verses on hand to hold up as truth when encountering challenges. God gives us one weapon to use to attack and advance against the enemy: his Word.

- God's Word, given through the Bible, gives children a foundation of truth that can make them strong in the face of adversity.

- The stories in the Bible teach children to trust the power of God working through them.

- Memorizing Bible verses arms children with truth when they face problems.

For the word of God is living and active,
sharper than any two-edged sword,
piercing to the division of soul and of spirit,
of joints and of marrow,
and discerning the thoughts and intentions of the heart.

HEBREWS 4:12

Lord God,

Your Word is truth. Give _____ and
_____ a love of your scripture that will last
throughout their lives. Let them know and love your stories and
wisdom in the Bible.

As _____ and _____ encounter
problems and hard times, use your Word like a sword, so they can
stand in truth, and experience your guidance and peace.

Give _____ and _____ Bible
stories to strengthen and grow them. Give them the words of Jesus
to teach them, and the wisdom of your scriptures to guide and
protect them.

Lead me with your Word. Let me take up this powerful
weapon daily to walk through my own life, confident and secure.

Thank you for giving us scripture and for the power and protection
that it brings to us.

Amen

❖

Everyone then who hears these words of mine
and does them will be like a wise man
who built his house on the rock.

MATTHEW 7:24

12

LET THEM PRAY

Children need to pray, and know people are praying for them.

praying at all times in the Spirit, with all prayer and supplication.

It is not surprising that Paul ends his list of protective elements with prayer. He encourages us to pray on all occasions with all kinds of prayer, and he asks for prayer for himself. Children need to know that they can connect with God in prayer.

To be effective, a soldier had to be in contact with his commanding officer. In the middle of the chaos of war the soldier could only see what was right in front of him. The commander had the bigger picture.

From higher ground the commander gave the soldier direction, and helped him make decisions that kept him safe and gave him success.
Even with all his armor and weapons a soldier

was ineffective without a plan. The plans were developed by those far away from the soldier. He was a small but essential part of a bigger plan.

Like a soldier is connected to his commanding officer, we can be connected to God, and we can help our children connect to God through prayer. He sees the bigger picture of our children's lives, and has a plan for each one of them. Through prayer God can direct and lead our children to safety and victory.

- Our children have an essential part to play in the world.

- They need to know that they can call out to their Heavenly Father for protection and guidance.

- As parents and caring adults in a child's life we must let our children hear us praying for them, and teach them to pray.

Continue steadfastly in prayer,
being watchful in it with thanksgiving.

COLOSSIANS 4:2

Lord,

Teach us to pray. Show us the power of connecting with you.

Honor the prayers that we have prayed for _____
and _____ these past weeks. We offer our prayers
for them knowing that you love our children and want the best for
them.

May they be strong with truth, righteousness, faith, service, peace,
salvation, scripture and prayer.

Help me to teach my children to pray. Give them the confidence that
you will hear them.

As I have prayed for these blessings for _____ and
_____, bless me too that I may know you and love
you and experience your protection.

Thank you for the people in my life who have prayed for me. Thank
you for giving me the honor of praying for _____
and _____.

Amen

❖

Out of my distress I called on the LORD;
the LORD answered me and set me free.

PSALM 118:5

13

KEEP THEM ON TRACK

Daily practices are necessary to maintain a child's faith.

keep alert with all perseverance

There are many distractions to pull our children away from faith and weaken their armor. Distractions compete with the time they devote to God. Without a way to stay on track our children can stray. For the full armor to be effective they need to maintain it.

The Roman soldier's armor had to be maintained to be useful. The metal plates were vulnerable to rust, and needed to be cleaned and polished daily. The leather strips that held everything together had to be oiled, so as not to become dry and brittle.

It wasn't enough to have the armor. It wasn't enough to put it on. It had to be carefully and regularly maintained. Daily use was hard on the leather straps and bindings. The soldier had to examine the breastplate carefully to see if the straps were weakening. Taking care of the armor took time.

Practice was important, too. Soldiers practiced with a sword and shield daily for about four hours. They practiced with a shield and sword twice as heavy as their own, so that when they went into battle, their sword and shield would feel light.

Daily practice gave the soldier the experience to handle his weapons with ease.

Children need the time and dedication to persevere in their faith and their walk with God.

- Putting on our armor and maintaining it is not a one-time event. It is a life-time effort.

- We should encourage our children to make time for their faith.

- As parents and caring adults we can model a life dedicated to our faith and walk with God.

Blessed is the man who remains steadfast under trial,
for when he has stood the test
he will receive the crown of life,
which God has promised to those who love him.

JAMES 1:12

Dear God,

Thank you for the powerful picture that Paul gives us comparing the soldier's armor to the tools that you give us for our protection. Just like armor must be maintained and cared for, we know that faith requires daily attention.

May _____ and _____ always keep these spiritual tools close and ready. Give them the desire to spend time with you, so that they will never have a time in their lives when they don't know that you are with them.

Bless them with time and energy to maintain their faith and to be strong in your might. Let _____ and _____ grow in their knowledge of your values, in their understanding of the Word, in their love for you.

As _____ and _____ go through life, may they always be aware of their need for you.

Guide me in my faith to know how to stay close to you and to maintain my own spiritual armor.

Amen

let us run with endurance the race that is set before us

HEBREWS 12:1

14

GIVE THEM VICTORY

God's strength will lead our children to victory.

that I may declare it boldly

When we pray for the armor of God for our children, we are praying for so much more. Like a stone dropped into a pond, the ripples of the knowledge of God go out from them. We pray for our children. They pray for other children, who pray for others. The armor of God's protection is given freely to all who request it. And in the end, there is victory.

Each soldier represented his legion, but also a family, a village, and a nation of citizens. The soldier put his armor on in battle to protect himself, and to achieve victory, but the victory was not for him alone.

Standing in battle in his armor, he represented a lot of people born and yet to come. The battle had consequences far beyond what happened on the battlefield that one day.

When the army was victorious, the soldiers would march in a glorious parade back into Rome with the spoils of war. People lined the road into the city, and cheered as they returned.

The soldier's victory belonged to them all. The battle was over, and the celebration had begun.

What a beautiful picture for us to hold onto as we end our devotions on The Armor of God. Our children are in a victory procession, proud and strong, protected by the armor of God.

- Our children can live secure in their faith, and can share that faith with others.

- God gives his love and protection freely to those who ask for it.

- As parents and caring adults in a child's life we can introduce our children and others to the gift of eternal life, and spiritual protection that God provides to those who seek him.

But thanks be to God,
who gives us the victory
through our Lord Jesus Christ.

1 CORINTHIANS 15:57

Dear Lord,

We claim victory today for _____ and
_____ . With your love and protection they have
truth, righteousness, peace, faith, salvation, and the Word.

Thank you for the belt of truth that you have given our children, and
that you are truth.

Thank you for the breastplate of righteousness, and that you are their
righteousness.

Thank you for shoes of the gospel of peace, for you are their peace.

Thank you for being a mighty shield around them, protecting them
from the enemies lies.

Thank you for being their hope and salvation like a helmet,
protecting their minds and thoughts.

Thank you for giving them your Word as sharp as any sword.

Bless _____ and _____ to be a
blessing to others, sharing with them the good news of Jesus and the
protection that he provides.

I lift up these prayers not only for _____ and
_____ , but for all your children that will learn
about you from them.

Amen

❖

But thanks be to God, who in Christ
always leads us in triumphal procession

2 CORINTHIANS 2:14

ABOUT THE AUTHORS

The Writing Sisters, Betsy Duffey and Laurie Myers, were born into a writing family, and began critiquing manuscripts at an early age for their mother, Newbery winner Betsy Byars. They went on to become authors of more than thirty-five children's novels written individually and with their mother.

When their mother retired they made a decision to use their writing skills to share their faith. Their first novel for adults, *The Shepherd's Song*, was published by Simon and Schuster's Howard Books. The first book of their prayer series, *The Lord is Their Shepherd: Praying Psalm 23 for Your Children*, was released spring of 2016.

www.WritingSisters.com

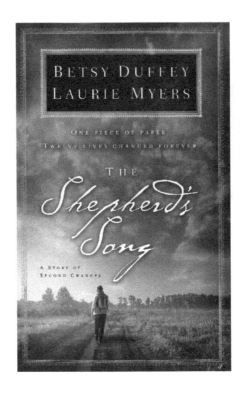

The Shepherd's Song:

A Story of Second Chances

Follow the incredible journey of one piece of paper—a copy of
Psalm 23—as it travels around the world, linking lives and hearts
with its simple but beautiful message.

With beautiful prose evocative of master storyteller Andy Andrews's
The Butterfly Effect, this story will touch your heart and remind you of
the ways God works through us to reach beyond what we can
imagine.

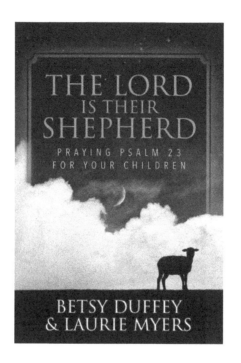

The Lord is Their Shepherd:

Praying Psalm 23 for Your Children

Quietly, a force of power is unleashed, changing the course of the world - the prayers of faithful women and men for their children. We will never be able to count the good choices made and bad choices avoided, bodies healed, lives grown in faith, as a result of these requests to God.

Do you sometimes wonder what to pray for your children? This guide, following Psalm 23, will help you. The book breaks down the beloved 23rd psalm into 14 devotions and prayers.